Know Jesus, Bless People

One Church's Commitment to Four Words

David Barker

Parson's Porch Books

www.parsonsporchbooks.com

Know Jesus, Bless People

ISBN: Softcover 978-1-949888-44-7

Copyright © 2018 by David Barker

All rights reserved. No part of this book may be reproduced or transmitted in any form or by any means, electronic or mechanical, including photocopying, recording, or by any information storage and retrieval system, without permission in writing from the publisher.

Know Jesus, Bless People

Contents

Introduction 7

Know Jesus 15
   In the Sauna with Horace

Bless the Community 28
   The Way of Wa

First Core Value: Shalom 40
   No Dollar General in Needles No More

Second Core Value: Compassion 53
   Choosing Compassion

Third Core Value: Grace 65
   The Chocolate Milkshake

Fourth Core Value: Integrity 80
   A Bar of Soap

Fifth Core Value: Community 93
   Every Who Down in Whoville

About the Author 105

Introduction

Field of Dreams says it all.

Ostensibly, it's a film about baseball or, on a slightly deeper level—and this should be no surprise given its title—a film about pursuing your dreams.

Yet it isn't really a film about baseball or dreams at all. If you read the novel on which the film is based, *Shoeless Joe* by W.P. Kinsella, you discover that baseball is a metaphor for faith, specifically Christianity, and Shoeless Joe Jackson, the real-life Chicago White Sox outfielder, is something of a Christ figure. And, speaking of metaphors, the decision made by Ray Kinsella (portrayed in the film by Kevin Costner) to plow under a huge chunk of his cornfield to create a baseball diamond can be seen as a metaphor for, literally, creating a significant place in your life for Jesus.

So when the voice tells Ray, "If you build it, he will come," he's not really talking about Shoeless Joe Jackson.

But Hollywood being Hollywood, any hint of Christianity was stripped from the story of *Field of Dreams*.

And yet…

At the end of the film, as the camera arcs up and away into the Iowa night sky, revealing streams of headlights, hundreds of cars, making their way to Ray's baseball field in pursuit of dreams of their own, suddenly the promise of *If you build it, he will come* seems overwhelmingly true.

Except it isn't. Not for Jesus, let alone for the church. Not anymore.

The days of building a church, hiring a pastor and staff and finding volunteer Sunday school teachers and Bible study leaders, and then opening the doors and people come because that's just what people do—those days are over. The so-called "attractional church" approach to following Jesus and growing the Kingdom that I was taught in seminary as little as 20 years ago simply doesn't work anymore. The church has become marginalized in its influence, often represented in the public square by its most extreme members. Among ever-growing numbers of people, the church is not seen merely as irrelevant and benign but as an active force for misogyny, homophobia, nationalism, and social regression. Among those demographics who in any way represent the church's future, the idea of awaking Sunday mornings, piling the kids in the car, and going to Sunday school and worship… well, that isn't even on their radar. A church can build the biggest buildings with the best preaching and teaching and worship and it pretty much won't matter: people *aren't* going to come, no matter what the voice promised.

My guess is that while the Lord may find this troubling, he doesn't find it surprising. Attractional church was never the plan anyway. Jesus' earthly ministry was not about building a building and staying put, expecting folks to show up, but about going out—out to where the people were, meeting them where and as they lived. And the history of the early church as narrated in the book of Acts and the letters of Paul and Peter and John tell a similar story. Yes, house churches were established, but the story of the burgeoning days of Jesus-followers was a story of relentless mission, people going out, rushing to keep up with a Holy Spirit that was busy preparing hearts and minds for the Gospel.

God, after all, is a missional God, a going-forth God, which, starting with Abraham, pursues a strategy of raising-up people as vehicles by which covenant promises, the work of the Kingdom, will bear fruit. Certainly, the Old Testament (and the New, for that matter) is rife with evidence of the strategy floundering in the weeds thanks to the missteps of a broken creation, but the strategy never altered. The *missio Dei*, the missional God, had a mission: redeem a broken creation... know Jesus as the Christ... be a blessing to all. And the church, for better or worse, was—and is—central to the mission.

For families of faith today, this tells us a lot. But most importantly, it tells us that a missional God is not well-served by an attractional church, and if attractional church is no longer working as a strategy for growing the Kingdom, we, like Jesus himself, should not be surprised. Nor should we continue with business as usual.

We need to change.

What follows is how one congregation, one family of faith, has come to understand and articulate that change. Being Presbyterians and therefore genetically predisposed to doing things Decently and In Order, we pursued a very systematic path of discerning what we call our Purpose and Core Values, a path we did our best to immerse in prayer and the study of Scripture, particularly in what we know as the Sermon on the Mount (Matthew 5-7). This was an important endeavor for those of us already calling CENTRALongmont Presbyterian Church in Longmont, Colorado home, but equally important for those we'll be laboring alongside as we work to bless our community. Should we be asked, "So, what are you and your church all about?", we wanted to be able to respond with something more than predestination and potlucks.

When I was interviewing for the pastoral vacancy here at CENTRALongmont, I was asked, "If we call you as our pastor, what will your dream be for us?"

I thought a moment, then told them, I don't so much have a dream for you as I have a dream for this community. My dream, I said, is this: one night, should there be a mini-Rapture and the entire congregation of Central Presbyterian Church is sucked up to Heaven, the next morning all of Longmont would gather around this building and *mourn*... mourn that we were no longer here because they realized what an incredible blessing this family of faith had been to the community.

Frankly, I think that's not a bad dream for every congregation to have.

TRANSFORMING CHURCH | TRANSFORMING LIVES | TRANSFORMING COMMUNITY

Purpose and Core Values

Our Purpose and Core Values are a distillation of our understanding of God's teaching. They are rooted specifically in Jesus' words in the Sermon on the Mount (Matthew 5-7).

Our **purpose** is to **know Jesus** and **bless our community**.

Our **core values** are

shalom... we work for wholeness, peace, and justice for all people

compassion... we extend mercy and understanding to all people

grace... we forgive as God forgives us

integrity... we live what we profess to believe

community… we're responsible for more than our own lives

As a distillation of our understanding of God's teaching, our purpose and core values direct everything we do. They are also a metric for evaluating how closely our actions match our beliefs.

Our purpose is **what** we do; our core values direct **how** we do what we do with each other, with our community, and with the world.

Know Jesus

In the Sauna with Horace

Jeremiah 4:19-22
Oh, my anguish, my anguish! I writhe in pain! Oh, the agony of my heart! My heart pounds within me, I cannot keep silent. For I have heard the sound of the trumpet; I have heard the battle cry. Disaster follows disaster; the whole land lies in ruins. In an instant my tents are destroyed, my shelter in a moment. How long must I see the battle standard and hear the sound of the trumpet? "My people are fools; they do not know me. They are senseless children; they have no understanding. They are skilled in doing evil; they know not how to do good."

1 John 2:3-6
Now by this we may be sure that we know him, if we obey his commandments. Whoever says, "I have come to know him," but does not obey his commandments, is a liar, and in such a person the truth does not exist; but whoever obeys his word, truly in this person the love of God has reached perfection. By this we may be sure that we are in him: whoever says, "I abide in him," ought to walk just as he walked.

John 10:11-15
"I am the good shepherd. The good shepherd lays down his life for the sheep. The hired hand, who is not the shepherd and does not own the sheep, sees the wolf coming and leaves the sheep and runs away—and the wolf snatches them and scatters them. The hired hand runs away because a hired hand does not care for the

sheep. I am the good shepherd. I know my own and my own know me, just as the Father knows me and I know the Father. And I lay down my life for the sheep."

Motion pictures have had a long history of analysis and criticism. I don't mean the kind you read in newspapers or *People* magazine or the *Rotten Tomatoes* website. Nor do I mean the kind written over the years by such recognized film critics as Rex Reed or Siskel and Ebert or Pauline Kael (not that such criticism doesn't have its place or serve its purpose). I'm talking about critical analysis of motion pictures and the motion picture industry by film scholars and historians, usually researching and working at colleges and universities. Much of the reason for this long history is because, early on, the motion picture was recognized as an *art form*, which gave it a certain status within academia. Which meant that films could acceptably be studied and analyzed with the same critical methods used to study literature and painting and music.

Television, on the other hand, though clearly having a more profound, more lasting impact on cultural and societal norms and behaviors, never had such a history. Television was always seen as low-culture, crassly commercial, mindless entertainment for the great, unwashed masses. A film—a work of art—you leave your home and pay money to experience it in a theater. There, in the dark, your entire focus (usually) is on the screen. You are drawn into a story that typically makes significant intellectual and emotional demands upon you.

But television…

Television was dismissed derisively as the "boob tube." You put your brain in neutral and idly flip through channel after channel, watching a minute or two of this program, a minute or two of that, all the while talking on your phone, playing with the dog, and making dinner. Innumerable studies were done over the years on the effects of television violence, but the idea of scholarly analysis of television narratives and aesthetics and the industry itself was laughable. Especially in academia, where scholars and researchers looked on the idea of serious television study as beneath contempt.

Until Horace Newcomb.

Horace Newcomb, a respected scholar with a PhD in English and American Studies, early in his career turned his very considerable attentions to television and, in doing so, pretty much single-handedly put the scholarly study of television on the academic map.

Horace was, without question, the foremost television scholar in the world... and a professor at the University of Texas at Austin... and, for five years, my mentor. He walked with me though my masters and doctoral program and co-directed my dissertation. Horace didn't just teach me how to study television and culture, Horace taught me how to think and he taught me how to write. If you've ever thought I had a way with words, if I've ever given you a new way of understanding anything, my ability to do so I owe largely to Horace Newcomb.

You also need to know this about Horace: I was absolutely terrified of him.

In the five years I spent under his tutelage, I got to know him well. At one time or another I read probably every word he'd ever written. He was demanding beyond belief, relentless in his criticism of my performance: nothing I did was ever good enough for him. The best grade he ever gave me was an A *minus*. Not to mention the fact that the sheer magnitude of his intellect—there seemed to be nothing that Horace didn't know more about than anyone else—intimidated me to the point that I was afraid to speak in front of him for fear I'd say something completely stupid. He hurt me, he made me feel woefully inadequate, he rarely had a positive thing to say about anything I did, and yet I idolized him. He was everything as a scholar and teacher I wanted to be yet knew I never would.

Then, one day, several years after I'd finished my doctorate and was a professor of television studies myself, the phone rang. It was Horace.

"David," he said, "I want you to come with me to Finland."

Horace had been hired as a consultant by YSL, the national broadcasting system in Finland, rather like the BBC in the UK.

"They want me to teach seminars on television narrative and aesthetics and production strategy," he explained. "I can't do it all myself, but you can do the aesthetics and production strategy stuff. The Finns will cover all your expenses plus an honorarium. You need to be in Helsinki next week."

Click.

I won't take the time now to explain the multitude of emotions I felt then. Suffice it to say that I spent a moment or two the next few days considering that I was going to be teaching the entire dramatic television department of Finnish National Broadcasting *while Horace Newcomb watched.*

My trip to Finland turned out to be one of the defining moments of my life, but not because I taught the entire dramatic television department of Finnish National Broadcasting while Horace Newcomb watched. It turned out to be a defining moment in my life because of something that happened one evening after dinner in an apartment block in a suburb of Helsinki.

Horace and I had been invited to dinner at the home of a YSL television producer by the name of Risto. Land in Finland is limited and therefore expensive and therefore most Finns live not in detached, single-family homes but in apartment blocks. Risto's apartment was lovely, and so was the meal and, afterwards, Risto asked Horace and me if we'd like a *sauna*.

Now, you need to understand something about Finns and saunas. Saunas in Finland are, shall we say, group events. Here, if you live in an apartment, and you're going to get together with some neighbors, you probably go to, say, a common picnic area there in the complex, grill some burgers, drink a few beers, have a few laughs. In Finland, you take a sauna. For every X-number of units in an apartment block, there's a sauna. You gather there with your neighbors, sweat, and drink vodka.

And it is very common for all in the sauna to be absolutely *naked*.

Risto had a wife. Her name was Ula. Ula was from Sweden. The picture that comes to your mind when you think young, attractive, blond Swedish woman… that was Ula. However, when Risto asked, "Do you want to take a sauna?", my first thought was *not* being naked in a sauna with Ula. My first thought was being naked in a sauna with *Horace*. This man… my mentor… my professional idol… *naked*.

As it turned out, Ula did not join us in the sauna. But Horace and I, there we were, side-by-side on a wooden bench, flagellating ourselves with tree limbs, naked as the day we were born. And, let me tell you: as well as I knew Horace Newcomb *prior* to that sauna, *after* that sauna, I knew him in a *completely* different way.

The lesson being, my brothers and sisters in Christ, that there is knowing someone, and then there is *knowing* someone…

The Hebrew word is *yada*. Its basic root meaning is *to know*. Given the extraordinary elasticity of biblical Hebrew, however, there are any number of nuances for *yada*. It can be a verb, it can be a noun. It can mean "knowledge," it can mean "cunning." It can even mean *wizard* or *fortune teller*. In Scripture, though, more often than not, *yada* means that basic root meaning: *to know*. But, as being buck naked in a Finnish sauna with your mentor reminds us, there is knowing and there is *knowing*. And when *yada* is used with reference to God, either our knowledge of God or God's knowledge of us, there is an added dimension. The dimension of *intimacy*.

In Jeremiah 4, after Jeremiah has given voice to the Israelite's anguish, God says in verse 22, *My people are foolish, they do not **know** me*. God is not saying the Israelites don't know *about* God, don't possess knowledge *of* God. God is saying the Israelites do not know God *intimately*, do not know God in such a way that they know God's heart, God's character, God's innermost desires for them. The knowing in question, therefore, is a knowing of profound intimacy, which is why, not coincidentally, *yada* is also the Hebrew word for sexual intercourse, as in, "Adam knew Eve his wife."

It is a similar situation with biblical Greek where the word for *to know* is *ginosko*. While Greek doesn't have quite the elasticity of Hebrew, there are nuances here as well, nuances that become clear in 1 John 2:3-6 and the John 10:11-15. In John's Gospel, Jesus uses the metaphor of shepherd and sheep, and providing we don't take it literally that Jesus regards his followers as mere sheep, we find something remarkable being said here. If we know Jesus with that profoundly intimate knowing, we not only can discern *his* voice from all other voices calling us, but *we* will know *him* as *he*, Jesus, knows the *Father*. Which is why, in the passage from 1 John, we're told that in truly knowing Jesus our behavior, our thoughts, our very lives will mimic his.

In other words, we're called to know Jesus so intimately that *our* lives become an expression of *his* life as *his* life was an expression of the *Father's* life. To know Jesus this way, in other words, is to have the life of Jesus within you.

To really begin to grasp the ramifications of what we're saying here, we need to do a little theology, and, as we all know, a little theology from time to time is good for the soul.

You may remember the Nicene Creed, which we recite occasionally (though probably not as much as we should) and that it says,

> *We believe in one Lord, Jesus Christ, the only Son of God, eternally begotten of the Father, God from God, Light from Light, true God from true God, begotten, not made, of one Being with the Father.*

Notice the "begotten" part: *"begotten, not made, of one Being with the Father..."*

This is not poetry. It's theology. Incredibly important theology, because it tells us that Jesus was not made by God from some sort of Jesus-stuff existing apart from God but was *begotten of* God. Which is to say, made from the very same essence as God Godself. God and Jesus, therefore, are of the same substance, as is the Holy Spirit. Theologians call this *homoousios*, and it's important because it's the foundation of our doctrine of the Trinity: God, Jesus, Holy Spirit, one essence in three forms, each fully the other. But for what we're about in discussing our Purpose as a family of faith, the real importance is this: the call to know Jesus is the call to be in such intimate relationship with the Lord that you come to know God as fully as a finite mind can possibly comprehend an infinite Deity. *Not* know *about... know*. *Not* book knowledge of Jesus... *sauna* knowledge of Jesus. Think of it this way: if book knowledge of Jesus and God is sufficient, the incarnation is unnecessary. Discipleship—what it means to follow Jesus—could be a course of study, and transformation—the real promise of the Gospel—a matter of reading a book.

It is absolutely no coincidence that the very first words of our purpose as a family of faith are these:

Know Jesus. The very first because there is *nothing* more important than *to know* Jesus, and by *know* we don't mean *head* knowledge. If that's all discipleship is about, if all it means to follow Jesus is to read books and go to classes, then discipleship *could* be a course of study. And the transformation piece… Well, in my experience, at least, no lasting transformation, no life-altering change of behavior can come merely by reading a book. Not even the Bible. At least, not the magnitude of change Jesus and the Kingdom demand because they're simply too difficult apart from the intimate relationship that comes *only* from truly knowing Jesus.

Now don't hear what I'm not saying.

By no means am I anti-intellectual or in any way denigrating the importance of learning all we can learn about Jesus and the Kingdom. But a broken world doesn't need more educated Christians. A broken world needs more educated Christians who've proactively moved beyond knowing *about* Jesus, to *knowing* Jesus. Because *knowing* Jesus results in transformation… in changed lives, changed thinking, and changed behavior. Which is how justice and equality and peace and love—the very essence of the Kingdom and Jesus' teachings—get done.

And it takes time, and we're not all in the same place, but that's why we say every week, no matter who you are, no matter where you are on your faith journey, you are welcome here. That you will be accepted, you will be loved, that we will make this journey together.

After taking the sauna with Risto and Horace, the three of us sat on the steps of the apartment block—fully clothed, thank you—where Ula met us with a bowl of strawberries that she'd just picked from the community garden behind the apartments.

If you've never eaten strawberries in Finland, you've missed one of the great blessings of life. You see, whatever it is in soil that strawberry plants use to make strawberries, there's more of it in the soil in Finland than anywhere in the world, which means Finnish strawberries taste more strawberry-y than any others. Until you've tasted them, you really cannot imagine how amazing they are.

As I'd headed to the sauna, I was truly afraid I might be scarred for life by what was about to happen. But sitting on the steps, eating strawberries, the sweet, red juice dripping down my chin and into my lap, I didn't feel scarred. I felt *affirmed*. Yes, there was the sauna, but during the ten days I spent in Finland, Horace, for the first time, talked with me not as a student but as a colleague... as a friend. He told me things about himself, about his life, about insecurities and anxieties that it never occurred to me someone like Horace Newcomb, television scholar extraordinaire, could ever have.

So in getting to know Horace, a knowing which, ultimately, had nothing to do with physical nakedness, it didn't make him any less an idol to me. He didn't become *less* Horace.

He became *more* Horace.

In getting to really know Horace, *I* became *more* David.

Which is, after all, what truly coming to know someone should do.

Bless the Community

The Way of Wa

Jeremiah 29:4-7

Thus says the LORD of hosts, the God of Israel, to all the exiles whom I have sent into exile from Jerusalem to Babylon: Build houses and live in them; plant gardens and eat what they produce. Take wives and have sons and daughters; take wives for your sons, and give your daughters in marriage, that they may bear sons and daughters; multiply there, and do not decrease. But seek the welfare of the city where I have sent you into exile, and pray to the LORD on its behalf, for in its welfare you will find your welfare.

John 8:12

Again Jesus spoke to them, saying, "I am the light of the world. Whoever follows me will never walk in darkness but will have the light of life."

Matthew 5:14-16

"You are the light of the world. A city built on a hill cannot be hid. No one after lighting a lamp puts it under the bushel basket, but on the lampstand, and it gives light to all in the house. In the same way, let your light shine before others, so that they may see your good works and give glory to your Father in heaven."

L et me begin by sharing some stats about Ichiro Suzuki or, as he's known to most fans of Major League baseball, just Ichiro.

Ichiro has played 26 seasons of professional baseball, nine with Orix Blue Wave of the Nippon Professional Baseball league in his native Japan, and 17 in Major League baseball here in the States. Most of those 17 years were with the Seattle Mariners but he also played for the Yankees and, most recently, the Miami Marlins.

Ichiro holds Major League baseball's record for most hits in a single season: 262. He has had 10 consecutive 200-hit seasons, the longest streak by any player in history in the MLB, and he has the most hits of any foreign-born player. Between his major league career in Japan and the United States he has the most hits of *any* player *period*. He has had seven hitting streaks of 20 or more games—the longest being 27 games— setting an American League record. In his 26 seasons, Ichiro has received 17 consecutive selections to the All-Star team and 17 consecutive seasons winning a Gold Glove. He has won nine league batting titles and Most Valuable Player four times. In his rookie season with the Mariners, he led the American League in batting average and stolen bases and was named Rookie of the Year and Most Valuable Player. In the 2007 All Star game, Ichiro won MVP for his three-hit performance, including the first inside-the-park home run in All Star game history. He leads all active players with 2,440 singles. He leads all active players in stolen bases with 508. In 2016 alone, he had batting, slugging, and on-base percentages all above .300 *and* he got his 3000th hit—off Chris Rusin of the Rockies at Coors Field... sorry, Rockies fans—all at the age of 43.

Now, if you know nothing whatsoever about baseball, trust me: these statistics are staggering... and Ichiro did it all without performance enhancing drugs, abusing his spouse, or holding out for the biggest contract in professional baseball history.

In his book, *The Meaning of Ichiro*, Robert Whiting writes about something the Japanese call *wa*, which means "group harmony," and it' a moral principle fundamental to Japanese society. *Wa* likely grew out of two realities: that Japan is a small island country with limited land and a country that, for centuries, was largely agricultural. Cooperation among farmers was imperative in order to ensure enough land, irrigation, and crops to feed the population. And the people themselves, given their number and the relative lack of living space, had to work with and for one another in order to survive. Throughout Japan's history, therefore, *wa* became critical to how the Japanese understood themselves as individuals and as members of a community. Never more so than after World War II when Japan rebuilt its economy—and society—from scratch. Every aspect of corporate culture became infused by *wa*, from consensus-based decision-making to promotions to elevator etiquette… to baseball.

It's often been remarked that the Japanese mania for baseball is a curious thing. How is it that the national pass-time of the United States became a national obsession for the Japanese? Yet, if you understand *wa*, you understand why a culture where individuals have their own identities but always in service to the group would be so mesmerized by the ultimate team sport. American football, by contrast, has never attracted much interest in Japan. Being a sport where players feel compelled to celebrate even the simplest play with look-at-me theatrics, American football is embarrassing to people who honor a game where after a player makes the most incredible play, he simply jogs to the dugout and perhaps, if it was a truly *spectacular* play, tips his hat.

In Japan, certain high schools are known as baseball schools. To be accepted into one of these schools not only puts a player on the fast track to professional ball but, because in Japan baseball is considered to be a supreme character builder, also results in the player later in life becoming a prime candidate for employment with Japan's largest corporations. Players in these schools follow a training regimen the equal of any pro ball training camp. They carry a full high school course load followed by baseball practice every weekday from 3:30 in the afternoon until 9:00 at night and all day Saturday and Sunday, for 11 months out of the year. They are given January off to go home and visit their families. And, through it all, *wa*: it's not about you, it's about the team… it's not about what *you* can do, it's about what you can do for the *team*.

Ichiro attended one of the most prestigious of these baseball schools, where he embraced, and was embraced by, *wa*. So every time he walked to the plate, whether in high school or in the major leagues, he wasn't swinging for the fence, thinking, *get a home run*.

Instead, he was thinking, *get a hit*… get on base… move the base runners… help the team.

Which explains why Ichiro has the stats Ichiro has.

In the book of Acts, barely 5 chapters in to the narrative of the early church, right after we're told that the believers were of one heart and soul, sharing all they had that all were provided for, we meet Ananias and Sapphira. Ananias and Sapphira had a piece of property they sold and then told Peter and the other Apostles that they were giving to the church all the money they'd made from the sale. But they were lying, and Peter and the others knew they were lying. Ananias and Sapphira had kept a portion of the money for themselves.

This story (and the verses just before it about the believers sharing all they had) is often used to further an ideological agenda: see, the early believers were Communists… they were Socialists. Or it's used to take a potshot at people with money: see, if you're stingy and don't give away more of your money, you're a sinner. But this story isn't really about politics or money at all; it's about *community*. Peter and the Apostles aren't particularly angry that Ananias and Sapphira held back some of the money they made from selling their property. Peter himself says, it was their property and, once they sold it, their money to do with what they pleased. Peter and the Apostles were angry because, first, Ananias and Sapphira lied about what they'd done. But, even more, they were angry because Ananias and Sapphira didn't understand—or failed to have faith in—one of the basic principles of the Kingdom. The basic principle that says, if you take care of the community you, too, will be taken care of. It's when we only care for ourselves, when we only care for the community minimally if at all, that people suffer.

This is the foundational truth behind Jeremiah's words to the Israelites in 29:4-7. Remember that when Jeremiah speaks these words to the Israelites, the Israelites are in Babylon. They are in exile, survivors of the siege of Jerusalem, living among the very people who besieged them. They are not in Israel, in their own communities, living and working and playing only among their own people. And yet look at what Jeremiah tells them to do: build houses... plant gardens... take wives... have children... give your children in marriage... have grandchildren... *multiply*. The Israelites, Jeremiah says, are to seek the welfare of the community where they are because as the community is blessed, they, the Israelites will be blessed. Don't, in other words, put your own well-being ahead of that of others.

Focus on *wa*.

Were we to look page-by-page through the Gospels, we'd find Jesus confronting individuals, teaching individuals, and healing individuals but always in service to something bigger than the individual's own wellbeing. How often did Jesus, in confronting, in teaching, in healing, follow with some variation on, "Now that you've been blessed, go forth and bless others..." And the reason Jesus did this is simple: while salvation and transformation may be about the individual, the Kingdom is about *community*, and we are saved and transformed not merely for our own eternal lives and spiritual nurture but to do the work of *community*.

Why? Why is the Kingdom—why was Jesus, why was the early church—so focused on community? In terms of the early church, no doubt, part of the reason for the focus was logistical and, from time to time, part of the reason for the focus was, frankly, safety. They weren't always pursuing their faith in the most hospitable of circumstances. But the real reason for such a focus on community was—and is—much more profound, and it begins with the nature of God Godself.

First, you'll remember Scripture tells us that God is love, that love is the very essence of God's being. But love requires an object. You don't just *love*… you love some*one* or some*thing*. Not even God can love apart from an object of that love. This is the primary reason for creation to begin with. God created that there might be an object for God's love. Furthermore, the nature of true love is not binding or limiting. It's *expansive*. It flows outward, it grows. It's not meant for us alone or for us and one other. Love, therefore, requires not only relationship; love requires community.

But even prior to creation, God modeled perfect community. In what we know as the Godhead—God, Jesus, Holy Spirit—they exist in perfect relationship, in perfect community with one another. Theologians and the so-called early church fathers used a word to describe this: *perichoresis*, a Greek word that refers to complete interpenetration, a kind of perfect, loving indwelling. And it can also mean, curiously enough, *dance*, so that, early on, the Trinity began to be represented visually by an image of God, Jesus, and Holy Spirit, arms intertwined, dancing with one another in a perfect circle.

What God desires for all creation, therefore, is to experience the love that can only be known in community, the love that cannot be found, let alone lived, alone, but only in relationship with others, in a community that embraces all creation. A love, a community that mirrors *perichoresis*, a community of such love and acceptance and equality that it can be spoken of in terms of interpenetration. Which is to say, a community where each individual sees every other individual as a brother or sister and it is recognized that the well-being of one can only come as a consequence of the well-being of all. Or, put another way, if one individual suffers, the entire community suffers. This is what God intends human life to be, an intention that many in the world—and in this country—have clearly lost sight of if, indeed, they've ever understood it at all. And because it's what God intends explains why Jesus and the Kingdom are so utterly focused upon it.

Jesus says, *I* am the light of the world… *you* are the light of the world. Jesus is not talking about wattage. Jesus is talking about an understanding of how we, as human beings, are to live, and how the world, as God's creation, is to be. It is a remarkable, frightening, humbling claim: you and I, as followers of Jesus, are to be to the world as Jesus was to the world. Not that we *are* Jesus, that, somehow, we're saviors or healers or in any way divine as Jesus was, but that we are to model for the world how Jesus tells us to live. Which means that the community God desires to embrace *all* creation *must* start with us.

This is the answer to the question, "In looking at the world about us right this moment and knowing Jesus, what's next? What should we do?" We are to work to create that kind of all-loving, all-inclusive, all-compassionate community where what comes first is not a country but the Kingdom.

Which is why the second half of our Purpose as a family of faith is what it is: to Know Jesus is not only to know the light of the world but to know that we, too, are to be that light to others, that we are to *bless the community*. As Jesus himself said:

Let your light shine before others so that they may see your good works and give glory to your Father in heaven.

As Jesus himself said:

Love God and love others as you love yourself.

In 2003, a player for the Tokyo Giants by the name of Masahiro Kawai did something during a game, and when he did, the game came to a complete stop. Fireworks shot into the sky beyond the centerfield wall, and as the capacity crowd in the stadium erupted in cheers, Kawai's family joined him on the field where they were all showered with flowers. Kawai had not pitched a perfect game or a no-hitter... he was an infielder. He'd not set a record for homeruns... in point of fact, Kawai was not a great hitter. What Kawai had done was lay down a perfect sacrifice bunt... the 514th sacrifice bunt of his career, thereby setting the record for most sacrifice bunts ever by a major league player.

Now, if you don't know baseball, a sacrifice bunt is a hit that drops the ball somewhere in front of home plate. Its sole purpose is to advance the runners already on base. The player who makes the bunt can virtually always count on being thrown out at first base and then jog back to the dugout.

Kawai's coach was quoted after the game saying, "The Japanese love to sacrifice for the team. It's considered an honor."

I will close as I began, with a statistic: in any given season, in professional baseball in Japan, there are three times as many sacrifice bunts as in Major League Baseball in America.

There's a message in that statistic for us as a country. There's a message in that statistic for us as a church.

First Core Value: Shalom

No Dollar General in Needles No More

Ezekiel 34:25-31

> *I will make with them a covenant of peace and banish wild animals from the land, so that they may live in the wild and sleep in the woods securely. I will make them and the region around my hill a blessing; and I will send down the showers in their season; they shall be showers of blessing. The trees of the field shall yield their fruit, and the earth shall yield its increase. They shall be secure on their soil; and they shall know that I am the LORD, when I break the bars of their yoke, and save them from the hands of those who enslaved them. They shall no more be plunder for the nations, nor shall the animals of the land devour them; they shall live in safety, and no one shall make them afraid. I will provide for them a splendid vegetation so that they shall no more be consumed with hunger in the land, and no longer suffer the insults of the nations. They shall know that I, the LORD their God, am with them, and that they, the house of Israel, are my people, says the Lord GOD. You are my sheep, the sheep of my pasture and I am your God, says the Lord GOD.*

Ephesians 2:11-22

So then, remember that at one time you Gentiles by birth, called "the uncircumcision" by those who are called "the circumcision"—a physical circumcision made in the flesh by human hands remember that you were at that time without Christ, being aliens from the commonwealth of Israel, and strangers to the covenants of promise, having no hope and without God in the world. But now in Christ Jesus you who once were far off have been brought near by the blood of Christ. For he is our peace; in his flesh he has made both groups into one and has broken down the dividing wall, that is, the hostility between us. He has abolished the law with its commandments and ordinances, that he might create in himself one new humanity in place of the two, thus making peace, and might reconcile both groups to God in one body through the cross, thus putting to death that hostility through it. So he came and proclaimed peace to you who were far off and peace to those who were near; for through him both of us have access in one Spirit to the Father. So then you are no longer strangers and aliens, but you are citizens with the saints and also members of the household of God, built upon the foundation of the apostles and prophets, with Christ Jesus himself as the cornerstone. In him the whole structure is joined together and grows into a holy temple in the Lord; in whom you also are built together spiritually into a dwelling place for God.

I want to talk about the first of our Core Values as a family of faith—*shalom*—by telling you a story. A story about a town of 4000 people on the California side of the Colorado River in the Mojave Desert named Needles.

Standing in the middle of Needles, depending on which direction you look, you'd either be 200 miles northwest of Phoenix, 100 miles southeast of Las Vegas, or 250 miles pretty much due east of Los Angeles. Were you to look right around you, at Needles itself, you'd see a town that is slowly but inexorably dying.

Named for the needle-pointed mountain peaks nearby, Needles, thanks to the Atchison, Topeka and Santa Fe, was founded in 1883 as a railroad town. During the Dust Bowl in the 1930s, it's location on Route 66 made it an important stopping point for homeless mid-westerners on their way to California. Eventually, however, the fact Needles was just across the river from Arizona became its undoing. Higher corporate tax rates and much more stringent building codes in California meant larger businesses such as Walmart and Home Depot built not where you are in Needles but in Bullhead City, Arizona, a 20-minute drive across the river. No one takes the train to Needles anymore and gasoline is a dollar-a-gallon cheaper on the Arizona side of the river. So, one day, the Needles Dollar General store closed its doors and put a sign in the window: *Going Out of Business*.

A three-hour drive west of Needles, the Dollar General store going out of business caught the attention of Aaron Moore. Moore is a graduate of Fuller Seminary in Pasadena. The shelves in his office are full of books on philosophy and theology, and shelves without books hold his collection of Near Eastern pottery. A Bible lies open on his desk. Moore is not a pastor, nor is he a professor. He is, however, a native of Hesperia, California, which is the headquarters of the place Moore went to work immediately upon graduation from seminary: The Victor Valley Transit Authority. Moore's job title is Director of Consolidated Transportation Services.

The Victor Valley Transit Authority has responsibility for mass transit throughout the 34,000 square miles of Victor Valley and being responsible for it was never part of Moore's vocational plans. His vocational plans *did* involve becoming a professor, but then he took a seminary class in missiology—the study of mission—where he was taught that ministry was less about bringing stuff to people than it was about opening up opportunities for them to see God's love. Moore began volunteering at Fuller's food bank which provides food to any in Pasadena who need it. It wasn't long before he noticed a pattern among regular users of the food bank: if they didn't show up one week, rarely was it because they didn't need food but almost always because they couldn't afford the transportation to get there. Moore realized that services like the food bank don't much matter if the people who need them can't get to them. Helping people get to the services they need, therefore, could be its own form of ministry, and if people were falling through the gaps in a densely populated city like Pasadena, Moore wondered what must be happening in a sparsely populated area like Victor Valley where most towns are small and the distance between them significant.

So it was that after graduation Moore found himself not behind a pulpit but in front of the Board of Directors of Victor Valley Transportation Authority charged with finding creative ways to get people where they needed to be. And he did.

Moore assembled a team and under his direction they implemented numerous programs, such as donating used cars to churches and non-profits who use them to connect people to health care, after-school programs, and church services. Or a driver reimbursement program that refunds costs to volunteers who drive people in the community to appointments and other services, a program with the added benefit, by the way, of building community as neighbors get to meet one another.

Running errands, shopping, doctor visits… These are basic things we take for granted, Moore says, but they're things most of us cannot do without transportation, and anxiety about transportation increases anxiety about social realities in general. The longer I do this job, Moore says, the more I realize transportation is at the center of so many challenges a community faces: poverty, mental health, isolation, access to health care…

Which is why the day Moore heard that the Needles Dollar General store was closing, it caught his attention. He knew that the only source of inexpensive food for many people in Needles was, for better or worse, the Dollar General store. The store closing meant people would go hungry. So Moore and his team developed a rideshare program so that families in Needles could carpool to nearby towns that still had a Dollar General. Ultimately, Moore says, it's not about transportation but about helping people live. But not just *live*. But live knowing they matter to others, that others care about them and will be there for them.

Now: what does this tell us about *shalom*?

Scripture is clear: God's intent for humanity is that we not be alone but live in community, in harmony, and in security, each of us focused, always, on the joy and well-being of all. Which means that *all* people are children of a single family, heirs to the same hope and the same destiny: to thrive, and to help care for one another and for God's creation. God's vision for creation, therefore—a vision that is foundational to everything else in Scripture—is a vision of joy, harmony, prosperity, love, loyalty, truth, grace, salvation, justice, blessing, righteousness.

Collectively, this is *shalom*. Peace, which is the way *shalom* is so often translated, is certainly part of what *shalom* is about, but even more it's about *wholeness*, with everything that implies. We should pay close attention to the language of Ezekiel 34:25-31. "Covenant of peace," it says… live and sleep securely… blessing… fruitful… deliverance from bondage… justice… safety… no hunger… no thirst… no threats from others… The picture that Ezekiel paints is a picture of what God intends creation to be, a picture of *shalom*. A picture of peace, yes, but not peace as the world understands it—absence of conflict—but as *God* understands it: justice, compassion, *wholeness*. All summarized in that final, extraordinary image of caring and comfort, that we will be the sheep of God' pasture and God will be our God, an image foundational to the characterization throughout Scripture of God... of Jesus... as the Good Shepherd.

We have pointed out on more than one occasion that, thanks to the world's understanding of peace, God's understanding is so often dismissed as short-sighted and naïve.

And yet, *shalom* is our best—our *only*—hope for the future of a broken creation, which is why Paul says what he does to the Ephesians in 2:11-22. Apart from community under the Lordship of Christ, Paul says, we are lost. As long as we're servants to an understanding of life rooted in the values and priorities of the world, we cannot have—the world cannot have—that for which we were created: *shalom*. Paul tells us *Jesus* is our *shalom*, and the result of being in that *shalom*, is the creation, literally, of a new humanity. Look at what Paul says:

So he—that is, Jesus—*came and proclaimed peace to you who were far off and peace to those who were near; for through him both of us have access in one Spirit to the Father. So then you are no longer strangers and aliens, but citizens with the saints and members of the household of God...*

This is language that resonates with Scripture's vision of creation from the very beginning, that, indeed, creation is to be *one*, every creature living with every other creature in community, focused on the joy and well-being of all.

But, my sisters and brothers in Christ, *shalom* does not rain down upon us like manna. To whatever extent *shalom* could be a gift from God, the truth is that *shalom* really only happens to the extent you and I are willing to live as Jesus calls us to live. There are no shortcuts to *shalom*, yet it is the pursuit of shortcuts that seems to consume us. Jesus modeled and taught *shalom*, but, as we know, truly following his example requires most of us to change how we understand the world and how we live. And the change, as we also know, is not easy, so we look for shortcuts, for ways of living, of being that, we say, "work for me." Ways that, typically, are far less demanding than those modeled and taught by Jesus. In the process, however, elements of *shalom*—elements like security or prosperity or justice—usually become something different, and what they become says less about Jesus and the Kingdom and more about our own politics, priorities, and lifestyles.

My guess is that Aaron Moore's job would be much easier if he simply focused on bus routes and cost effectiveness, if he simply said, "The greatest demand from the greatest number of people is to be able to get from point A to point B and from point C to point D. So if this bus at this time gets you to your doctor appointment or to the bank or to the store, terrific. If not, we can't help you. It's not our responsibility nor do we have the resources to meet everyone's specific needs, no matter how basic."

But Aaron Moore doesn't do that. He doesn't understand the Kingdom in terms of the demands of his job. He understands the demands of his job in terms of the Kingdom. The ministry Aaron Moore does in Victor Valley reminds us that *shalom* cannot be the outcome of market forces. It cannot be subject to profit and loss statements. It can't be legislated or executive ordered. The ministry Aaron Moore does in Victor Valley reminds us that *shalom* can only truly happen when people put the Kingdom before themselves.

So it is that, as a family of faith, *shalom* is one of our Core Values, and the fact it is foundational to so much else Scripture teaches us is why it's our *first* Core Value. But as we move from an understanding of our Purpose as a family of faith to our specific Core Values as a family of faith, we need to understand a few things about Core Values in general, about what makes a Core Value *core* rather than just a value.

First, *Core Values are non-negotiable.*

They are not subject to how we vote or whom we love. We don't get to take them up or put them down as the mood strikes us, nor remake them according to what we find comfortable or convenient. And this is so because these values are not *our* expectations of one another, they are *Jesus'* expectations of *us*.

Second, *Core Values are not goals, they are realities.*

We don't strive for our Core Values, we live them. They aren't something we hope to achieve in the future, they are something we live now.

And third, *Core Values are both prescriptive and diagnostic.*

They both tell us what to do and enable us to discern the correctness of what we're doing.

All of which means each of us should be in constant engagement with our Core Values: are we being the people Jesus calls us to be and the Kingdom expects?

So let's get very concrete.

In terms of *shalom*, if we're not seeing *all* people as our brothers and sisters and doing what we can as we can for equality and justice and wholeness and peace as Jesus defines and models these, then—no more shortcuts—we've got work to do. And if the thought of taking on the second half of that statement—

equality and justice and wholeness and peace—
overwhelms us, then let's start with the first. Because
equality and justice and wholeness and peace cannot
be apart from each of us first seeing all people as
brothers and sisters in the family of God, we must
never forget that working for the betterment of
people apart from seeing everyone as brother and
sister does not result in *shalom* but in what we see so
much of in the world around us: segregation and
inequality, sexism and racism. I will work for *my*
betterment, and for the betterment of people like me,
but *you*—you're on your own.

The challenge that presents is that even if *we* don't
love all people, God *does*. Jesus didn't just die for me
and people who think and act like me. Jesus died for
everyone. We therefore cannot call ourselves Jesus
followers if we're engaged in any action that separates
people into *us* and *them*. We cannot call ourselves
Jesus followers if, for example, we insist on making
what a person says or does inseparable from who they
are so that rather than judging their behavior we
demonize their very being. Part of the reason for the
cross is that we need never be defined by the worst
thing we've ever done. It is, ultimately, about *grace*,
must start with grace, because *apart* from grace, *shalom*
is just a noble idea.

So it is that to begin to live *shalom*, we must live *grace*.

Aaron Moore, not long after he began work at the Victor Valley Transit Authority, was asked how he understood his work. "I see my work as an expansion of Christ's body and the church," Moore responded. "It may be an impossible vision, but I want to see a day when everyone can get to where they need to go."

A day when *everyone* can get to where they need to go. That, my sisters and brothers in Christ, is as good a metaphor for *shalom* as I know.

Second Core Value: Compassion

Choosing Compassion

Zechariah 7:8-10
The word of the LORD came to Zechariah, saying: Thus says the LORD of hosts: Render true judgments, show kindness and mercy to one another; do not oppress the widow, the orphan, the alien, or the poor; and do not devise evil in your hearts against one another.

Matthew 9:35-38
Then Jesus went about all the cities and villages, teaching in their synagogues, and proclaiming the good news of the kingdom, and curing every disease and every sickness. When he saw the crowds, he had compassion for them, because they were harassed and helpless, like sheep without a shepherd. Then he said to his disciples, "The harvest is plentiful, but the laborers are few; therefore ask the Lord of the harvest to send out laborers into his harvest."

A week ago Saturday here at the church, we held a funeral, or, as we refer to it in the Presbyterian Church, a Service of Witness to the Resurrection. There is a pattern to these services, a pattern which includes, a few minutes before the service begins, the family gathering in Fellowship Hall to join hands in a circle and pray together. We'd formed the circle,

Know Jesus, Bless People

taken one another's hands, and I was just opening my mouth to pray when in the door walked a man. He wasn't a member of the family, there for the prayer, or someone attending the service who'd happened to turn left instead of right, ending up in Fellowship Hall rather than the Sanctuary. He was a homeless man. I recognized him. He'd been in the church before. He walked to where we were standing and everyone in the circle turned to look at him. He started to hold out his hands as if he intended to join our circle which, I remember thinking, could be awkward, so I asked him, "Can I help you?" He quietly said something about wanting to talk to a pastor. "I'm sorry," I said, "but we're about to begin a funeral service. I can't talk right now."

He apologized, backed away and left. I prayed, and because I then had to focus on the service, forgot about him.

The next day, Sunday, worship over, I went into Fellowship Hall and picked up a piece of the cake there for the baptism we'd just celebrated. I was putting the second bite in my mouth when I saw him: the homeless man from the day before, threading his way through groups of people, headed for me.

"Do you remember me?" he asked.

"I do," I said.

"You snapped at me yesterday," he said. "All I wanted to do was talk."

I started to explain again why *then* hadn't been a good time to talk, but before I said more than two words, he began talking. He told me he was born and grew up in California, that he'd married a woman and, together, they had three kids but then his wife became pregnant by another man so he left her, and that ever since he left, his kids would have nothing to do with him, and how much it hurt that they treated him as they did.

At one point, when he paused to take a breath, I asked him if he needed anything, any kind of help.

"No," he answered, "no, I don't. I don't ask anybody for anything."

And he picked up where he left off, that he'd come to Longmont because there were people he knew here but that it was better he lived alone and since he couldn't afford rent he lived in his car…

I'm standing there, in one hand a plate with a piece of cake missing two bites, in the other, a fork, because it somehow didn't seem right to eat cake in front of a man who lives in his car, and I began listening less to what he was saying and thinking more about the meeting I was late to and the class to sit in on after the meeting, and he kept talking, and I was getting antsy, wondering how much longer this would go on when he didn't really need anything but just wanted to talk and how could I get out of this gracefully when something occurred to me and I asked him if he'd like a piece of cake and he said sure and when he turned to step over to the table where the cake was, I saw my chance and turned away.

Someone else—a church member—was there, wanting to talk to me, so we talked a minute and then another church member came up and *we* talked a minute, and I was able to finish my cake. And without looking back, I made my way to the door, down the stairs, and to the meeting. And when the meeting was over, to the class. And when the class was over, to my office and then to my car and then I was on my way home… on my way home, thinking about the morning. Thinking about preaching *shalom*, about wholeness and joy and peace for all people, and was the sermon good and did I do a good job delivering it and did people like it, and that next week I'd be preaching about compassion. And I thought about baptizing those two beautiful little girls, a baptism which was also a celebration that two beautiful little girls had been adopted from foster care by parents who loved and cherished them and would provide them a home and everything they'd ever need.

And then I thought about a homeless man… a homeless man who lived in a car and had children who wouldn't even speak to him… and all he wanted from me was to listen.

Most of us, I think, tend to assume that morality—specifically our inclination to help other people, our inclination to be compassionate—is a function of religious conviction, or of how we were raised. And while undoubtedly there is truth in such an assumption, much research has been done which suggests the inclination to be compassionate is a good deal more complicated than religion and raising. That as much as compassion is a consequence of forces external to us—the church, our parents—compassion is equally, perhaps even more, a consequence of forces *within* us: of biology… DNA… evolution. In fact, research suggests that at the most basic levels of survival, compassion evolved in humans to ensure self- and group preservation. Put another way, from an evolutionary perspective, compassion is built to enable groups to survive, not to achieve world peace.

Thus, the behavioral and brain function studies that indicate we humans are wired to, first, take care of and look out for ourselves as individuals and for the group to which we belong, which helps explain the human propensity for dividing people into *us* and *them*. And that it is not necessarily our natural inclination to look out for and care about people *outside* our group, however we define said group, because *they* are competing with *us* for the same resources, for survival.

Further, research indicates this inclination to look out for and care about others varies both culturally and regionally. A group in one place will have a different understanding than a group in another place of what people, especially strangers, owe one another. We see this, for example, in the differences in hospitality codes from one culture to another.

All of which allows me to conclude that if I run into that homeless man again, I can explain my behavior toward him as not really my fault at all but a consequence of evolution. I can tell him that, in fact, he should be grateful I was as patient as I was. He isn't, after all, one of *us*, part of the group that is CENTRALongmont, not to mention the fact that I *did* give him a piece of cake.

I *could* conclude that. But I know better.

Research can provide an *explanation* for my behavior, but all the research in the world cannot provide an *excuse* for my behavior. The fact is that compassion is a choice, and in the case of this man, I did not choose compassion. The choice I *did* make wasn't made maliciously. I'm pretty confident I didn't actually snap at him Saturday, and Sunday I was tired. It had been a challenging and stressful week and, as on all Sunday mornings, I had a lot to do. Still, I made the choice I made.

Perhaps the fact that from an evolutionary perspective, we're more wired for self- and group protection than world peace explains why all the world's major religions have one fundamental belief in common. Be you Buddhist, Jewish, Muslim, Hindu, Taoist, or Christian, your faith embraces the same fundamental tenet: *do unto others as you would have them do unto you.*

The fundamental tenet embraced by all the world's major religions, therefore, is *compassion*, which, by definition, involves others, because compassion requires we put ourselves in the place of another human being. Not merely to *sympathize*, which is something you can do from a distance: "Oh, I feel terrible about what's happening to you…" But *empathize*, which means we put ourselves, to the fullest extent we can, in their place, feel what they feel, and are then moved to take action to address it. In compassion there can be no *us* and *them*, only us, which is not to eradicate or diminish difference among peoples but to acknowledge that within the difference is a common humanity.

Think about Jesus: walking all over the Galilean countryside, tired and challenged and stressed and more to do than time to do it in. He's been teaching and healing for weeks and seeing still more crowds of people who need him. His choice was never merely sympathy, or some pretense he was listening when, in fact, he was thinking about the next town he had to get to. His choice was never merely to tell someone, "I feel your pain... I hope you're better soon," then go back to eating his cake. His choice was *compassion*... to stop... to truly be present and listen... to teach when there was a lesson to be taught... to heal when there was a wound to be healed... and, always, to love.

Now, true enough, compassion was a rather different sort of choice for Jesus than it is for us. While fully human, Jesus was also fully divine. Jesus embodied love and mercy in a way we mere mortals never can, could heal in ways we can't, teach in ways we can't, solve problems in ways we can't, understand people in ways we can't. But that isn't really the point, is it? That you and I aren't Jesus is a pretty lame excuse for not doing what Jesus calls us to do. We're not expected to *be* Jesus, only to be the most *like* Jesus we can be and being the most like Jesus we can be means to always do our best to choose *compassion*.

I think that maximizing our ability to always choose compassion involves several things.

First, I think it requires that we live from a mindset of *abundance* rather than scarcity.

If, indeed, our evolutionary inheritance is to privilege ourselves and our group over others because they are competing with us for the same resources, that would explain why we tend to think in terms of scarcity, that there *isn't* enough to go around. Such thinking undergirds much of life in Western society in particular; in our economics, for sure, but also in our openness—or lack thereof—to including others in our way of life. It also informs how we distinguish *rights* from *privileges*. Part of how we understand what people deserve, what we are entitled to, involves our perceptions of whether or not there's enough to go around. But while it is true that some resources are finite, in the economy of the Kingdom there is always enough for all *if* all have only what they *need*, as opposed to what they want… or what they can.

Second, I think that choosing compassion requires we withhold judgment.

Judgment is almost always an exercise in control and self-protection. If I see someone—say, a man walking into Fellowship Hall—and based solely upon the way they look, think, *homeless* and, then, if I check off all the preconceived attributes I carry around in my head about what *homeless* means—dirty, broke, lazy, drunk, drug addict, head case, threatening—not only does it relieve me of any responsibility to invest the energy necessary to actually get to know them, it allows me to categorize them as something I don't want to get involved with. That they are a *them*, not an *us*, so I can turn my back, look the other way, walk off. Judgment short-circuits empathy, which means compassion then doesn't have a chance.

Third, I think choosing compassion requires us to educate ourselves about people rather than relying on fears and stereotypes and prejudices.

As Daniel Patrick Moynihan famously said to a fellow Senator, "You are entitled to your own opinions, but you are not entitled to your own facts." Consider, for example, Dreamers... people whose future in this country has become a hotly-debated issue. I often hear people say that Dreamers don't deserve compassion because they're law-breakers. They may have had no control over the fact their parents brought them to this country when they were children, the argument goes, but now that they're adults, they ought to begin the process of obtaining legal citizenship. But such thinking is based on ignorance of the law. To begin the process of obtaining citizenship, you have to have a Green Card, which is to say be a legal permanent resident, and Dreamers are not eligible for Green Cards.

And, lastly, I think compassion requires grace.

The Golden Rule embraced by all faiths, *do unto others as you'd have them do unto you…* What is that but an admonition to grace?

Fred Rogers was often criticized for what some perceived as a sappy and naïve view of human beings, a view given voice in every episode of *Mister Roger's Neighborhood*…

> *You always make each day a special day…*
> *and you know how?*
> *By just being you—I like you just the way you are.*

Rogers once answered his critics this way:

> *Love isn't a perfect state of caring. It's an active noun like "struggle." To love someone is to strive to accept that person exactly the way he or she is, right here and now. No one is so perfect there's no room for them to improve as people. But we all need to know that we're*

loved as we are, regardless of who we are or what we've done.

Every single worship service at CENTRALongmont begins with all of us together saying, *whoever you are, you are welcome here…*

Welcome, as I obviously forgot last Saturday, is not just a word we say on Sunday, and in saying *welcome*, we aren't just extending a greeting, because the *welcome* we say means far more than just *hello*. It means that no matter your color, your ethnicity, your gender identification, whom you love, your dress, how you talk, how you smell, we will honor you as a brother or sister in Christ. You will find acceptance here. You will find understanding here. You will find community here and grace here and love here, because *compassion* is a Core Value here.

Do we always get it right? Clearly, no. Starting with me, we don't always get it right. But if each of us focuses first on doing what we know is right before focusing on what others are doing we believe to be wrong, we can be more compassionate people.

Third Core Value: Grace

The Chocolate Milkshake

Ephesians 2:1-10

> *You were dead through the trespasses and sins in which you once lived, following the course of this world, following the ruler of the power of the air, the spirit that is now at work among those who are disobedient. All of us once lived among them in the passions of our flesh, following the desires of flesh and senses, and we were by nature children of wrath, like everyone else. But God, who is rich in mercy, out of the great love with which he loved us even when we were dead through our trespasses, made us alive together with Christ—by grace you have been saved—and raised us up with him and seated us with him in the heavenly places in Christ Jesus, so that in the ages to come he might show the immeasurable riches of his grace in kindness toward us in Christ Jesus. For by grace you have been saved through faith, and this is not your own doing; it is the gift of God—not the result of works, so that no one may boast. For we are what he has made us, created in Christ Jesus for good works, which God prepared beforehand to be our way of life.*

Matthew 18:21-35

Then Peter came and said to him, "Lord, if another member of the church sins against me, how often should I forgive? As many as seven times?" Jesus said to him, "Not seven times, but, I tell you, seventy-seven times. For this reason the kingdom of heaven may be compared to a king who wished to settle accounts with his slaves. When he began the reckoning, one who owed him ten thousand talents was brought to him; and, as he could not pay, his lord ordered him to be sold, together with his wife and children and all his possessions, and payment to be made. So the slave fell on his knees before him, saying, 'Have patience with me, and I will pay you everything.' And out of pity for him, the lord of that slave released him and forgave him the debt. But that same slave, as he went out, came upon one of his fellow slaves who owed him a hundred denarii; and seizing him by the throat, he said, 'Pay what you owe.' Then his fellow slave fell down and pleaded with him, 'Have patience with me, and I will pay you.' But he refused; then he went and threw him into prison until he would pay the debt. When his fellow slaves saw what had happened, they were greatly distressed, and they went and reported to their lord all that had taken place. Then his lord summoned him and said to him, 'You wicked slave! I forgave you all that debt because you pleaded with me. Should you not have had mercy on your fellow slave, as I had mercy on you?' And in anger his lord handed him over to be tortured until he would pay his entire debt. So my heavenly Father will also do to every one of you, if you do not forgive your brother or sister from your heart."

Rwanda, sandwiched among Uganda, Tanzania, Burundi, and the Democratic Republic of the Congo, is one of the smallest countries in Africa, barely 10,000 square miles. Rwanda gained independence in 1962 but within 30 years a civil war broke out between the two peoples making up the vast majority of the Rwandan population, the Hutu, who held the power in the country, and the Tutsi. In 1994, the Hutu government engineered a genocidal slaughter of Tutsi, in a 100-day period from early April to mid-July murdering as many as 1,000,000 people. The killings were done by members of the Rwandan army, government-backed militias, and, very often, neighbors. Hutu were incited to murder their Tutsi neighbors, which they did. Most did not use guns for the killing as you might expect because most didn't have guns. Instead, they used what they did have: machetes. By the time the genocide ended, 70% of the Tutsi population had been killed, and 30% of a pigmy people, the Batwa.

Several decades after the genocide, a non-governmental agency was formed: The *Association Modest et Innocent*, literally the "Modest and Innocent

Association," although they're better known by the acronym AMI, after the French word for *friend*. AMI formed small groups of Hutus who perpetrated the genocide and Tutsis whose families were victims of the genocide. They were counseled over many months, culminating in the perpetrator formally asking the victim for forgiveness. If the victim agreed to forgive the perpetrator, the perpetrator and his family—the perpetrators were almost all men—typically brought a basket of offerings to the victim, usually food and sorghum or banana beer, and the perpetrator and victim sealed the forgiveness by singing and dancing together.

The photo is of Jean-Pierre Karenzi and Viviane Nyiramana. One day, during the genocide, Jean-Pierre

and several other men took machetes and murdered Viviane's father and three brothers and then burned Viviane's house to the ground. Speaking of Jean-Pierre, Viviane said, "He did these killings, but he alone came to me and asked my forgiveness. Then he and other men who'd been in prison for killing came and built me a house with a covered roof. I was afraid of him, but I forgave him, and now in my mind I feel peace…"

Scripture, in both the Old and New Testaments, speaks of grace in multiple ways, with multiple words but, mostly, it speaks of grace in two ways: in terms of deliverance or salvation and in terms of forgiveness.

By grace you have been saved through faith.

These words from the 8th verse of the second chapter of Ephesians were the words that opened the eyes of Martin Luther to the reality that there was nothing he could do to earn salvation, that it was a gift, completely unmerited, given by a gracious God. Words that, probably more than any other, ushered in what we know as the Protestant Reformation; words… a promise… fulfilled over and over again throughout the Scriptural witness, that in spite of our sins, in spite of our brokenness, in spite of our continual embrace of the ways of the world rather than the ways of the Kingdom, our salvation is assured. Through our faith in Christ Jesus, by the gift of a gracious God, we can be delivered from the death of sin to new life. We can be made whole, at one with God, grafted into the body of Christ. And even our faith in Jesus is not entirely of our own doing but a gift of grace, enabled by the work and power of the Holy Spirit within us. On our own, therefore, there is nothing we can do to earn the grace of God.

For many of our sisters and brothers in Christ, salvation by grace through faith is the Holy Grail of the faith. The primary goal of claiming Jesus Christ as Lord and Savior, as they see it, is salvation. Yet, salvation, important as it is, was never intended to be solely an end unto itself because as much as our salvation is about eternal life, it is about life here and now.

Salvation doesn't just reserve us a table in Heaven; it begins the process of transformation, the remaking of our lives such that we each are more nearly like Jesus. Which means that the grace, the forgiveness *we've* received from God we are to extend to one another.

Jesus himself makes this clear. In the Sermon on the Mount, Jesus tells us that before we get down to the business of worshiping God we need to make sure we've dealt with anyone we need to forgive or who needs to forgive us. When Peter asks Jesus if forgiving someone seven times is enough, Jesus responds no, you should forgive them 70 times 7—a bit of hyperbole to make the point that you should never stop forgiving. And when teaching the disciples how to pray, Jesus makes the centerpiece of prayer these words: ... *and forgive us our debts as we forgive our debtors.*

But nowhere are Jesus' expectations about grace and forgiveness given stronger voice than in the parable in Matthew 18:21-35.

To fully appreciate the magnitude of the grace the unforgiving servant receives from his master, we need to understand something about the money involved. The unforgiving servant, we're told, is in debt to his master the King for 10,000 talents. A talent was, during Jesus' time, the largest monetary unit available: one talent was worth 6,000 drachmas. Six-thousand drachmas is what a laborer like the unforgiving servant would make in 15 years. Which means it would take the unforgiving servant 150,000 years to pay off the debt... providing, of course, there was no interest being added to the principal in the meantime. Jesus' point is that the master forgave the servant a debt the servant could not possibly repay. The debt that the slave owed the unforgiving servant, on the other hand—one hundred denarii—was equivalent to three months wages. The unforgiving servant, in other words, having just been forgiven a debt he couldn't pay off in 150,000 years was unwilling to forgive a debt that could have been paid off in three months.

But Jesus' words are not really about money and debt. Jesus is talking about grace and forgiveness. You who have been forgiven so much, Jesus is saying, are to extend grace to and forgive one another in just the same way. And the grace and forgiveness of which Jesus speaks doesn't just come into play as a consequence of something that happens to us directly. The grace and forgiveness of which Jesus speaks also applies to people and situations and behaviors that do not happen to us directly but that we merely observe happening from a distance.

If you are like me, the reach of your judgment extends far beyond people and situations that affect you directly. You watch TV, read the paper, look at your Facebook feed… you see things that you think are wrong, people who aren't behaving the way you think they ought to behave, and even though the wrong in question is, as the old saying goes, no skin off your nose, you still judge and criticize… right? We have a hard time extending grace to someone who cuts us off in traffic; what about a King who forgives his servant a debt the servant couldn't repay in 2,000 lifetimes? What about a woman who forgives the man who hacked her husband and three brothers to death with a machete and then burned her house down? What are we to make of them?

Bryan Stevenson is the founder of the Equal Justice Initiative, a legal practice in Alabama dedicated to defending the poor and wrongly condemned throughout the South. In his profound and moving book, *Just Mercy,* Stevenson tells the story of his first visit with Avery Jenkins, a mentally-challenged man on death row for murder.

As Stevenson, who is African-American, pulled into the prison parking lot, he saw a pick-up truck which, in his words, "looked like a shrine to the Old South." The truck was covered in Confederate flag decals and pro-gun and Southern identity bumper stickers, one of which in particular caught Stevenson's attention: *If I'd known it was going to be like this, I'd have picked my own damn cotton.*

When Stevenson entered the prison, he was met by a correctional officer he'd never seen there before, a white man, muscular build, early 40s, short military haircut. Stevenson walked toward the gate that led to the lobby of the visitation room where he expected the routine pat-down all attorneys received, but the officer stepped in front of him and snarled, "What are you doing?" When Stevenson explained why he was there, the officer told him, "If you expect to get in *my* prison, you're going to the bathroom and taking everything off."

Stevenson pointed out that attorneys are not subject to strip-search but that just made the officer angrier: "I don't know who you think you are, but you can get in that bathroom and strip or you can go back where you came from." Stevenson went to the bathroom, removed his clothes, and the officer searched him—roughly. Dressed again, Stevenson told the officer he'd like to go into the visitation room. The officer said, "First you have to sign the book." The book, used to log family visitations, was not used for legal visits. "I don't have to sign the book," Stevenson said. "If you want to come into *my* prison," the officer responded, "you sign the book." Stevenson signed the book. Finally, the officer unlocked the door to the visitation room, but as Stevenson took a step forward, the officer grabbed him by the arm and stopped him. "Did you happen to see that pickup truck with a lot of bumper stickers, flags, and a gun rack?" he asked. Stevenson said, yes. "I want you to know, that's my truck."

Finally in the visitation room, Stevenson's client, Avery Jenkins, came up to him and before Stevenson could introduce himself, said, "Did you bring me a chocolate milkshake?"

When Stevenson told him no, he didn't bring him a chocolate milkshake, Jenkins grew quiet and unresponsive, and it was only after Stevenson promised to bring him one the next visit that Jenkins began to answer Stevenson's questions.

Jenkins was calm and soft-spoken but, Stevenson writes, clearly mentally ill. Yet mental illness was never even mentioned during his murder trial. Stevenson looked into Jenkins' history and what he found, in Stevenson's words, was heartbreaking. Jenkins' father had been murdered before Jenkins was born. His mother died of a drug overdose before he was a year old. He was in foster care by his second birthday, living in 19 different homes by the time he was eight. By the age of ten he was with foster parents who abused him, locking him in a closet and starving and beating him as punishment. One day his foster mother took him out in the woods, tied him to a tree, and left him there. He was found by some hunters three days later. After recovering from serious medical problems resulting from his abandonment, he was turned over to authorities who put him back in foster care. By the age of 13, Jenkins was abusing drugs and alcohol; by 15, he was having seizures and psychotic episodes; by 17, he was deemed "incapable of management" and put out on the streets, homeless. He was in and out of jail until he turned 20 when, in the midst of a psychotic episode, he stabbed to death a man he thought was a demon trying to kill him. Jenkin's lawyers did no investigation of his history. He was quickly convicted of murder and sentenced to death.

Stevenson worked for months to get Jenkins a new trial, meeting with his client regularly, who began every visit with the same question: *Did you bring me a chocolate milkshake?* and, every visit, Stevenson having to tell him no because the prison wouldn't allow it.

Eventually, Stevenson was able to gain a hearing before a judge to request a new trial. Jenkins was present in the courtroom, each day brought from the prison to the hearing by the correctional officer who drove the pick-up truck. For three days, Stevenson presented expert witnesses who detailed how organic brain damage, schizophrenia, and bipolar disorder can result in severe mental impairment which, in turn, can result in dangerous behavior. He also presented testimony about how the foster care system had failed Jenkins, passing him from one damaging situation to the next until he was drug addicted and homeless. Stevenson felt good about the hearing even though he knew that in the South a postconviction hearing rarely resulted in a favorable ruling.

About a month later, before a ruling had been handed down, Stevenson decided to visit Jenkins to see how he was doing. When Stevenson arrived at the prison, he was greeted by the same correctional officer.

"I'll just go into the bathroom to prepare for the search," Stevenson said.

"Mr. Stevenson," the officer replied, "you don't have to worry about that… I know you're OK."

"Well, I'll go sign the book then," Stevenson said.

"Mr. Stevenson," the officer responded, "I saw you coming and signed it for you."

Stevenson, surprised and confused by this complete change in the officer's attitude, thanked him, then walked to the visitation room door. Before letting him in the room, the officer placed a hand on Stevenson's shoulder and said, "There's something I'd like to tell you.

"You know I took Avery to court every day for his hearing. While I was there, I was listening. It was difficult stuff for me to hear. I came up in foster care and didn't think anybody had it as bad as me. They moved me around like I wasn't wanted nowhere. I had it pretty rough. But listening to what you were saying about Avery made me realize there were other people who had it worse than I did. I got so angry growing up there were plenty of times when I really wanted to hurt somebody just because I was angry. Sitting in that courtroom brought back memories, and I think I realized how I'm still kind of angry. I guess what I'm trying to say is that I think it's good, what you're doing... you done good for Avery... really good...

"One other thing I want you to know. I did something I probably shouldn't have done, but after the last day of the hearing, on the way back here to the prison, I exited off the interstate, and I bought Avery a chocolate milkshake."

The third of our Core Values as a family of faith is *grace*... that we forgive as God forgives us.

If we can't imagine how you go about forgiving the person who took a machete and hacked your husband and brothers to death and then burned your house to the ground... if we see that and think, how is it possible to forgive that?

If we encounter Jesus' command that we forgive and never stop forgiving and think, who really can live that way?

If we read a story where a King forgives a debt so great it can never be repaid, and know that's what God did for all humanity through Jesus' death on the cross, and argue, well, after all, that was God, and we're not God…

Maybe we *can* begin to forgive others as God forgives us by putting aside some of our anger, some of our bitterness over our own wounds that we might better see the wounds of others. That we be willing to feel some measure of compassion, because it's from compassion for the pain of others that we can begin to forgive the pain others have caused us.

Shortly after Bryan Stevenson entered the visitation room, Avery Jenkins appeared. As always, Stevenson began by apologizing he couldn't bring him a chocolate milkshake, but Jenkins cut him off.

"I got my milkshake," Jenkins said, smiling. "I'm OK now…"

Avery Jenkins was granted a new trial which resulted in him being released from death row and placed in a facility where he could receive mental health treatment. And never again did he ask Stevenson for a chocolate milkshake.

Fourth Core Value: Integrity

A Bar of Soap

Proverbs 21:2-3

All deeds are right in the sight of the doer, but the LORD weighs the heart. To do righteousness and justice is more acceptable to the LORD than sacrifice.

Matthew 5:17-20; 7:21-29

"Do not think that I have come to abolish the law or the prophets; I have come not to abolish but to fulfill. For truly I tell you, until heaven and earth pass away, not one letter, not one stroke of a letter, will pass from the law until all is accomplished. Therefore, whoever breaks one of the least of these commandments, and teaches others to do the same, will be called least in the kingdom of heaven; but whoever does them and teaches them will be called great in the kingdom of heaven. For I tell you, unless your righteousness exceeds that of the scribes and Pharisees, you will never enter the kingdom of heaven."

"Not everyone who says to me, 'Lord, Lord,' will enter the kingdom of heaven, but only the one who does the will of my Father in heaven. On that day many will say to me, 'Lord, Lord, did we not prophesy in your name, and cast out demons in your name, and do many deeds

of power in your name?' Then I will declare to them, 'I never knew you; go away from me, you evildoers.'

Everyone then who hears these words of mine and acts on them will be like a wise man who built his house on rock. The rain fell, the floods came, and the winds blew and beat on that house, but it did not fall, because it had been founded on rock. And everyone who hears these words of mine and does not act on them will be like a foolish man who built his house on sand. The rain fell, and the floods came, and the winds blew and beat against that house, and it fell—and great was its fall!" Now when Jesus had finished saying these things, the crowds were astounded at his teaching, for he taught them as one having authority, and not as their scribes.

I want to begin by asking a question: was… *is*… Jesus a Christian?

We'll save an answer for later.

The fourth of our five Core Values as a family of faith is *integrity*, we live what we profess to believe.

If you Google *integrity* and *Christian*, you discover a lot of on-line Bible studies concerning what Scripture says about integrity and why integrity is important to the Christian life. You also find a fair amount about integrity in business.

But you also discover a lot of hits on why Christians are such hypocrites. Much has been written, it seems, in response to the unfortunately widely-held perception that Christians *don't* practice what they preach. Many of the responses are, perhaps not surprisingly, defensive, and those that are frequently make the same two arguments. First, they argue that before you condemn Christians for being hypocrites you should remember that many people who claim to be Christians in fact are not, by which those making this argument usually mean that such people aren't the same stripe of Christian *they* are. I'm not entirely sure how to respond to this argument. It seems to me that in responding to a perception of hypocrisy, dismissing significant numbers of people as not somehow Christian enough could be counter-productive.

The second argument, on the other hand, strikes me as a good deal more insightful. This argument says that the ethical demands Jesus makes of his followers are impossibly high. Therefore, Christians, in terms of practicing what they preach, should not be criticized for falling short. *No one* can reasonably be expected to live as Jesus demands. What really matters, therefore, is how hard an individual Christian *tries* to practice what they preach.

Now, I said I found this second argument more insightful, but not, I suspect, for the reason intended by those who make it. This idea that Christians, called as we are to embrace an impossibly high moral and ethical standard, cannot help but fall short so cannot help but appear to non-Christians as being hypocritical, *is* widely embraced by many Christians— Including me, for much of my life. It's usually something we say in the same breath as grace… we all try, we all fall short, but, through God's grace, we're all forgiven. The important thing, as I said, is that we do our best, that we keep trying. But over time I've come to believe that not only does such an idea ultimately miss the point but that, in embracing it, we in fact set ourselves up for failure. A failure for which our communities, our nation… indeed, all God's creation… often pays a heavy price.

To explain what I mean, I want to talk about Nelson Mandela and a bar of soap.

Once, when Mandela was President of South Africa, he was on a diplomatic trip to Kuwait. Mandela noticed that, as was usually the case, the hotel room in which he was staying was stocked with an array of toiletries—shampoos, conditioners, soaps, etc.—and Mandela, as he usually did, took note of the number of each. Sometime later, Mandela noticed that a bar of soap was missing. He called together every member of the security detail that was staying with him at the hotel and told them a bar of soap was missing. Whoever took the soap has until the end of the day to return it, Mandela told them, and if it wasn't returned by the end of the day, every single one of them would be fired.

When I first encountered this story, as much as I admire Nelson Mandela, I thought to myself, that's ridiculous. It was a little bar of soap... soap provided by the hotel to be used. By whom shouldn't really matter. Besides, the hotel undoubtedly had thousands of other little bars of soap just like it if Mandela needed one. My wife Terry and I used to take the little bottles of shampoo and conditioner all the time and give them to our daughter Jessica because she thought they were cool. Surely Mandela's reaction—return the bar of soap or everyone loses their job—was over the top... *way* over the top.

But then I learned that Mandela wasn't as concerned about the act of taking the soap as he was about what the act represented, which was a way of thinking that rationalized a behavior such that a basically dishonest act—taking something that isn't yours—becomes acceptable. Yes, it was just a bar of soap, but the real issue for Mandela was the *integrity* of the individual who took it. It wasn't the behavior but the *belief behind* the behavior, a belief Mandela would not tolerate.

Thus, the problem with the conviction we all try, we all fall short, we're all forgiven.

In saying we know we need to practice what we preach but because the demands of the practice are so impossibly high we cannot help but fall short, what we're focusing on is *behavior*. Which is fine, as far as it goes. Christ-like behavior, obviously, is important. What we miss when we focus on behavior, however, is the *belief behind* the behavior, which leads us to the real challenge of Christians and integrity: the problem isn't that we don't live what we believe; the problem is that we *do* live what we believe.

Why is that a problem?

Because what we believe often has nothing to do with Jesus.

We fail in our attempts to live the way Jesus calls us to live not because his ethical and moral standards are impossible. We fail because our understanding of what it means to follow Jesus has more to do with worldly norms than with Jesus' teachings. In short, we will never *live* like Jesus until we *understand life* like Jesus and, in the meantime, we—and our communities and our nation and all God's creation—suffer.

This isn't cynicism. It's Scriptural reality. All deeds are right in the sight of the doer, Proverbs 21:2-3 says, but the Lord weighs the heart. Worldly creatures that we are, we can justify what we're doing as right, but God searches our hearts, looking for an understanding of right action that results in righteousness and justice. And Jesus himself ends the Sermon on the Mount—the blueprint for how we, as his followers, are to live—by saying that practicing what you preach is only going to work if what you preach is accurate to begin with. Right behavior can only follow from right understanding. You will live as I call you to live, Jesus essentially says, only once you understand the world as I call you to understand it.

This is why the first thing Jesus says when he emerges from the wilderness to begin his earthly ministry is *repent*. We hear that and think, *sin*... Jesus is telling us to stop sinning... and he is, but he is saying so much more than that. Sin—wrong behavior—is the result of wrong thinking. Stopping sinning, therefore, requires thinking in a new way. In saying *repent* what Jesus is saying is this: completely re-structure your hearts and minds... adopt, literally, a new consciousness, a new way of understanding life and the world. This is why Paul, writing to the Philippians (2:5), says "let the same mind be in you that was in Christ Jesus..." Why, in Romans, he says, "do not be conformed to this world but be transformed by the renewing of your minds so that you may discern what is the will of God" (12:2).

It is this transformation of our minds, my sisters and brothers in Christ, that we are missing. For the vast majority of people who call on Jesus Christ as Lord and Savior, we have not done the work of taking on the mind of Christ. What we've done instead is craft a version of Christianity filtered through our political, economic, cultural, and sexual beliefs. And, to the extent we know it at all, understand Scripture in ways compatible with how we prefer to live and believe the world should be. This explains how some can square Jesus' teachings on material wealth with free market capitalism while others square them with socialism. How some can square Jesus' teachings on human relationships with condemning same-sex relationships and others with embracing them. How some can square Jesus' teachings on our responsibilities to one another with deporting aliens and others with fully accepting them. It explains how Christians on all sides of any given issue—sexism, racism, nationalism, gun control, abortion, global warming, militarization… you name it… can be convinced *they* are right and everyone else is wrong. It explains why, for most of us, the version of Christianity we practice says far more about us as individuals than it does about Jesus and Scripture.

Which brings us back to the question I asked at the very beginning: Was... is... Jesus a Christian?

Well... *no*, he wasn't.

Jesus was Jesus. Christianity is what, over the centuries, we broken human beings have created in Jesus' name. The really hard truth, my sisters and brothers, is this: Jesus never calls us to be Christians... Jesus calls us to be Christ-like.

So the real question isn't, is Jesus a Christian? The real question is, am I Christ-like?

Our Core Values as a family of faith are our attempt to characterize Christ-like living, and of the Core Values, this one—integrity—once we really understand what it requires of us, may well be the most challenging. I'm not suggesting we're all lacking in integrity. I'm speaking now specifically in terms of integrity as it applies to our efforts to be Jesus followers, and I want to call our attention to something *really* important.

We have our Purpose and Core Values *everywhere*—you don't have to look very far to find them. We want to keep them in front of us as much as possible. Look at what it says after integrity: *we live what we profess to believe.*

These words are a very deliberate choice. Note that it *doesn't* say, we live what *we* believe. It says, we live what we *profess* to believe. It's the difference, my friends, between being Christian and being Christ-like. We're not striving to live into our *own* understanding of the world. We're striving to live into *Jesus'* understanding of the world, because it is *Jesus'* understanding we profess.

How? How do we live into Jesus' understanding? How do we be Christ-like as opposed to Christian? How do we achieve the same mind in ourselves as was in Jesus? How can we be transformed rather than conformed?

To begin with, we have to acknowledge that such understanding, such transformation ultimately will happen only by the work of the Holy Spirit. But that doesn't mean we're off the hook. We each have our own work to do, work that can only start with confession: my faith has more to do with me than with Jesus. Confession followed by commitment: to critically deconstruct all my assumptions and beliefs and biases and convictions, every intellectual and emotional construct that shapes what I believe. Then, once I do that, be willing to take each construct and ask, is this rooted in the world or in Jesus? And I can only recognize if they're rooted in Jesus if I actually know and understand what Jesus said.

Which raises the question for each of us: *How well do I really understand what the Bible says?*

Notice I'm saying *understand*, not *know*. There's a difference—and it's a difference that makes all the difference—between *knowing* what Scripture says and *understanding* what Scripture says.

And understanding requires *grappling*.

Grappling in that I approach Scripture not assuming I already know what it says or that the understanding I think I have is correct.

Grappling in that I don't just study Scripture with people who think exactly the way I do so rather than engaging in critical thinking I simply reinforce the biases I already have.

Grappling in that I'm reading Scripture continually, as a daily discipline, assuming I *don't* know what it means and seeking out multiple understandings from multiple points of view.

Grappling in that I'm reading Scripture not with the intent that *I'm* going to make *it* understandable but that *it* is going to make *me* understandable.

Next, I need to practice humility… I may be wrong. And along with humility, I need to practice grace.

The ordering of Core Values 3, 4, and 5 is not coincidental: grace comes from compassion, and humility—essential to integrity—comes from grace. I am continually astonished at how many brothers and sisters in the faith attack one another for not having grace, compassion, or humility in ways that are utterly lacking in grace, compassion, and humility. One of the biggest hindrances to the Holy Spirit transforming my mind is not only to think I'm always right, but to demonize and vilify those who think differently. The only cause advanced by rhetoric that demeans another human being is the further closing of my own mind.

Confess, commit, grapple, understand, be compassionate, give grace, be humble…

It's not a weekend project. It's a life-long journey that will end only when we're with Jesus and he says, "So, tell me… why did you call *me* Lord but lived like you were?" If the thought of the journey overwhelms me… I'm too tired, too stressed, too busy to take it on… if I'm convinced I've figured out a way of being a Christian that works for me so it's a journey I don't really need to take… so be it.

There are, after all, thousands of other bars of soap.

Fifth Core Value: Community

Every Who Down in Whoville

Genesis 1:26-27

Then God said, "Let us make humankind in our image, according to our likeness; and let them have dominion over the fish of the sea, and over the birds of the air, and over the cattle, and over all the wild animals of the earth, and over every creeping thing that creeps upon the earth." So, God created humankind in his image, in the image of God he created them; male and female he created them.

John 17:20-23

"I ask not only on behalf of these, but also on behalf of those who will believe in me through their word, that they may all be one. As you, Father, are in me and I am in you, may they also be in us, so that the world may believe that you have sent me. The glory that you have given me I have given them, so that they may be one, as we are one, I in them and you in me, that they may become completely one, so that the world may know that you have sent me and have loved them even as you have loved me.

Remember Dr. Seuss' *How the Grinch Stole Christmas?*

Every Who down in Who-ville liked Christmas a lot...

But the Grinch, who lived just north of Who-ville, did NOT!

The Grinch hated Christmas, the whole Christmas season!

Now, please don't ask why. No one quite knows the reason.

It could be his head wasn't screwed on just right.

It could be, perhaps, that his shoes were too tight.

But I think that the most likely reason of all

May have been that his heart was two sizes too small.

But whatever the reason, his heart or his shoes,

he stood there on Christmas Eve hating the Whos,

Staring down from his cave with a sour, Grinch frown,

At the warm lighted windows below in their town.

And the story, you'll recall, goes on to tell about the Grinch dressing-up like Santa Claus, descending from Mt. Crumpit with his dog Max, and going through Who-ville Christmas Eve night, house to house, stealing toys and stockings and Christmas trees and Christmas decorations... even the food for Christmas dinner. All in the name of preventing the Whos from celebrating Christmas with playing and laughing and eating and singing. Only for the Grinch to discover that in spite of his theft from the Whos of every outward expression of Christmas, rather than cry and wail as he'd hoped, they still joined hands and sang. Which twitterpated the Grinch no end. How could the Whos still be so happy? And then he realized: it wasn't the *what* that made the Whos joyful, it was the *who*...

Every Who down in Whoville, the tall and the small,

Was singing! Without any presents at all!

He HADN'T stopped Christmas from coming! IT CAME!

Somehow or other, it came just the same!

And the Grinch, with his grinch-feet ice-cold in the snow,

Stood puzzling and puzzling: "How could it be so?"

"It came without ribbons! It came without tags!"

"It came without packages, boxes or bags!"

And he puzzled three hours, till his puzzler was sore.

Then the Grinch thought of something he hadn't before!

"Maybe Christmas," he thought, "doesn't come from a store."

"Maybe Christmas... perhaps... means a little bit more!"

And what happened then? Well... in Whoville they say,

That the Grinch's small heart grew three sizes that day!

And the minute his heart didn't feel quite so tight,

He whizzed with his load through the bright morning light,

And he brought back the toys! And the food for the feast!

And he, HE HIMSELF! The Grinch carved the roast beast!

The African-American writer James Baldwin once said that people aren't judged and attacked because of *who* they are but because of *what* they are, because of how their humanity is characterized and categorized by others. By which Baldwin meant that so often what person A thinks of person B, how person A *treats* person B, is not based on person A really knowing *who* person B is but, instead, by person A looking at *what* person B is: what color are they? what country to they appear to come from? what religion do they adhere to? what gender are they? what neighborhood do they live in? what language do they speak? what person do they love? And then person A makes decisions about person B: will I respect them or not? trust them or not? want them living in my neighborhood or not? want them in my church or not?

Even if we don't consciously mean to do it, we do it. It's a behavior that seems almost automatic, a behavior, maybe, arising from the fight-or-flight reaction hardwired into our DNA.

After all, on any given day, we likely encounter more people we *don't* know for *who* they are, only for, based on our assumptions, *what* they are. For our own safety—do I stay put or do I run—we have to make assumptions about them in a split-second and, for better or worse, such assumptions involve color and country and religion and gender.

The challenge arises when the assumptions that inform split-second decisions about fight-or-flight come to shape our understanding of people in *all* situations, come to shape our understanding of our society and our nation and our community. Especially, I think, of our *community*. We can talk about societies and nations and, for that matter, states and regions, but in terms of day-in, day-out lived reality, our most concrete experience of other people is in our *community*. And, to the extent we understand community as a series of ever-expanding concentric circles—and, here at CENTRALongmont, we do—how we understand community significantly impacts how we understand our region, our state, our nation, our society, our world.

Which is why, as our fifth and final Core Value as a family of faith, when we talk about community, we very consciously say, we're responsible for more than our own lives. By which we mean that for all our apparent, outward differences—the *what*—in terms of the *who*, we are all the same.

This recognition is foundational to the Scriptural witness about how God intends human beings to be with one another, and it starts at the very beginning of creation.

God created humankind in God's image, which isn't to say that when we get to heaven and see God, God will have two legs, two arms, two eyes, two ears, two hands, two feet, one head, a five-o'clock shadow, and a stomach hanging over God's belt. Being created in the image of God is more nearly an expression of worth, that every human being, created by God, is sacred. That for all the particularities and eccentricities that make every human being unique, human identity is not rooted in the *what* of those particularities and eccentricities but in the *who* of beloved child of God.

It is no coincidence that Adam and Eve are simply a *who* until their disobedience in eating the apple introduces into the equation the *what* of self-consciousness, awareness of their differences—*one of these things is not like the others*, as they used to sing on *Sesame Street*—shame, a need to hide, to lie, to blame. So that, soon enough, the world is populated not with people who first see one another individually as sacred but as groups: Amalekites, Jebusites, Ninevites... Egyptians, Assyrians, Babylonians... Galileans and Samaritans... Sadducees and Pharisees... groups characterized and categorized... Who or Grinch.

Until Jesus comes along and says *no*.

Love one another as I've loved you, Jesus says.[1] *All* people are your neighbors, Jesus says, and you've responsibility for each one.[2] Love God, Jesus says, and love your neighbor as yourself.[3] And Jesus says these things because Jesus knew that, in the

---

[1] John 13:34

[2] Luke 10:25-37

[3] Matthew 22:34-40

Kingdom, while there are many different people, there's only *one* community, and the health of that community will rise or fall on the extent to which all people first and foremost see one another as sacred… as beloved children of God.

And, thus, the remarkable prayer Jesus prays in John 17. Jesus prays first for himself, then for his disciples, then for all people, and the prayer for all people (17:20-23) is unlike any other prayer of Jesus anywhere in Scripture…

> *As you, Father, are in me and I am in you, may they also be in us, so that the world may believe that you have sent me.*
>
> *The glory that you have given me I have given them, so that they may be one as we are one, I in them and you in me, that they may become completely one, so that the world may know that you have sent me and have loved them as you have loved me.*

My sisters and brothers in Christ, take a moment and let the full profundity of those words settle into your hearts and minds…

They are a description of Jesus' vision of *community*, a way of living in which you and I enter into the same relationship with God and Jesus that *they* have with one another. A way of living that results in a unity among all people that is like the unity of God and Jesus. A way of living that is the ultimate testimony that Jesus is who Jesus is—the Son of God—and that we are loved by God *exactly* as God loves Jesus. All because before I see you, understand you, know you as anything else, I know you as created in the image of, as a beloved child of, God.

Eric Liu is the son of Chinese immigrants. His parents came to the United States from Taiwan and settled in Poughkeepsie, New York where he was born and raised. Liu studied history at Yale, graduated from Harvard Law School, served as Deputy Assistant to President Clinton for Domestic Policy, and was Director of Legislative Affairs for the National Security Council. Currently he's a Senior Law Lecturer at the University of Washington School of Law and Executive Director of the Aspen Institute on Citizenship and American Identity.

Several years ago, Liu found himself reflecting on the ceremony where immigrants become American citizens, a ceremony where they take an oath ascribing to a set of vows about what, in the broadest sense, it means to be not just an American, but a member of a community. And Liu thought to himself, what would it look like for all of us to take a vow… people born here, people who make their way here at some point in their lives... each American to renew his or her civic vows. Thus was born a project Liu calls *Sworn Again America*. It's a simple idea. Liu goes to public places, sets up a podium, and gives people the opportunity to renew their commitment to citizenship:

I pledge to be an active American

to show up for others

to govern myself

to help govern my community

I recommit myself to my country's creed

to cherish liberty

as a responsibility

I pledge to serve

and to push my country:

when right, to be kept right;

when wrong, to be set right

Wherever my ancestors and I were born

I claim America

and I pledge to live like a citizen

It can be a dangerous thing to talk about citizenship and religion in the same breath. It can become all too easy to equate one with the other. It can also be dangerous, despite the good intentions behind it, to simply make the blanket statement that for all our differences, we are basically the same. Our differences, our diversity *is* important—critically important—and to say that, in the end, they don't really matter is not to accept the differences but to diminish them. Instead, we might say that it's *because* we're Americans, not in spite of it, that our diversity is so important. Instead, we might say that it's *because* we're each sacred, beloved children of God that in all our diversity we are sisters and brothers.

Such thinking is central to our understanding, as a family of faith, of community. Far too many sisters and brothers in the faith are like the Grinch, sitting atop Mt. Crumpit, looking down on every Who in Whoville, judging them for *what* they are rather than loving them for *who* they are. Too many sisters and brothers whose hearts, like their understanding of community, are several sizes too small. There would be benefit, no doubt, for all of us if all of us were *sworn again*, if we each recommitted ourselves to citizenship.

But there would, I suspect, be greater benefit still to remembering that our first citizenship is in the community of the Kingdom. Community in the Kingdom requires that our hearts grow bigger, not smaller. That we lead not with the *what* but with the *who*. That before our thoughts, let alone our actions, say anything else, they say this: you and I and *all* God's children are sacred.

About the Author

David Barker has a B.S., M.A., and Ph.D. in Communication from the University of Texas at Austin and an M.Div. from Austin Presbyterian Theological Seminary. He was a professor and administrator in higher education for 15 years prior to entering the ministry where he has served 17 years. He is currently Pastor and Head of Staff at CENTRALongmont Presbyterian Church in Longmont, Colorado. He loves the mountains, reading, music, cycling and—as proof we live by faith and not by sight—the Chicago Cubs. He's married and has two children.

www.ingramcontent.com/pod-product-compliance
Lightning Source LLC
Chambersburg PA
CBHW052159110526
44591CB00012B/2010